The Forward Book
of Poetry 2001

FORWARD PUBLISHING
LONDON

First published in Great Britain by
Forward Publishing · 84-86 Regent Street · London W1B 5DD
in association with
Faber and Faber · 3 Queen Square · London WC1N 3AU

ISBN 0 571 20579 8 (paperback)

Reprographics by Colourpath · London

Printed by Redwood Books Ltd
Kennet House · Kennet Way · Trowbridge · Wilts BA14 8RN

A CIP catalogue reference for this book
is available at the British Library.

To Ruby Elizabeth

Preface

NINE YEARS HAVE FLOWN BY since the first Forward Book of Poetry and
the first Forward Poetry Prizes. Through these nine years and nine
anthologies, an extraordinary blend of poets, both famous and unknown,
both in fashion and out, have graced these pages.

Nine poets have won the Forward Prize and have each benefited to
the tune of £10,000. Nine first-timers have also taken away £5,000 each
for their efforts in the Waterstone's Best First Collection category. Of
the nine winners of the Tolman Cunard £1,000 Prize for Best Individual
Poem, some have been stalwarts on the poetry scene, others fresh voices
to reappear in later anthologies with a collection of their own.

Framed around the Forward Prizes has been its sister in rhyme,
National Poetry Day. Celebrated in schools, offices, railway stations
or anywhere where a love of poetry can hold an audience, National
Poetry Day grows in strength and support. For a week it seems
one cannot get away from poetry on the airwaves and on our television
screens. Poetry seems to have ascended from dusty corners of
bookshops into the lives of us all.

We would not have the opportunity to celebrate such an event
without thanking all those behind the day and prizes. We would like to
thank Susan Limb and Lesley Miles at Waterstone's and Jeffery Tolman
at Tolman Cunard, our partners at the BBC, The Poetry Society,
Colman Getty, Faber and Faber, and everyone at Forward Publishing.
Most of all I would like to thank our judges for this year's prize: John
Walsh, Annalena McAfee, Brian Patten, Jo Shapcott and Bill Swainson.

I hope you enjoy it.

William Sieghart

Foreword

'A DEFINITION OF POETRY?' said an editor friend last year. 'Oh I
don't know. Epiphanies with sound effects? That's the best I can do.'
It struck me at the time as a serviceable, if risky, declaration; I can't
remember the last time anybody had the nerve to lay down any laws
about what readers, writers and critics expect poems to be. But if
there's one thing that judging the Forward Prize tells you, it's how
hopelessly inadequate such formulations are.

Submissions for the prize came from every quarter – from Christian
vanity publishers, Welsh collectives, gypsy presses, West Country
pamphleteers, along with the more orthodox verse *ateliers* of Seren,
Arc, Rockingham Press, Smith/Doorstop and the factories of
Bloodaxe, Cape, Carcanet, Faber and the others. They all came
tumbling in, the serious, grown-up, would-be-canonical collections
by established names, the earnest, confessional first outpourings, the
awkward squad of poems that were first published in magazines or
journals. They arrived singly in envelopes, then by the dozen in Jiffy
bags, then by the score in cardboard boxes the size of steamer trunks.

And after a while it became clear that British poetry now takes
such myriad forms, exists in such bafflingly heterogeneous idioms,
that it resists any attempt to nail it down: the endlessly elaborated
metaphor, the surreal narrative, the seventeen-section minimalist
epic, the rhythmical travelogue ('Structural beams spike from
baked earth mosques/In Burkina Faso . . .'), the shy and gathered
lyric, the improvisatory prose riff, the history-of-art meditation,
the post-Bunyan fable ('Heart journeys to a whorehouse to discuss
love . . .'), the high-table poison dart, the tough-guy syllabics ('It is
four in the morning, and one lamp strobes me in its stutter'), the
Dorothy-Parker-lite light verse, the Craig Raine two-line stanza,
like parted lips or air sandwiches, the chatty reminiscence of
childhood, the lists, the haiku. . .

Most of all, there was the New Epic. How could anyone try to
compare Douglas Dunn's nine-part, 172-page *The Donkey's Ears*,
or Fred D'Aguiar's *Bloodlines*, his ottava rima narrative of runaway
slaves, with the more crystalline ambitions of the one-off lyric?
Wasn't it like judging novels and short stories for the same award?

Could *The Donkey's Ears* be seen as a series of individual poems that share a theme (like *Birthday Letters*)? Or is it a single entity? And if so, is *Billy's Rain* by Hugo Williams a collection of poems, as it appears to be, or a single long poem, cunningly arrayed as separate lyrics? Should there be a separate prize for the *verse-novella*?

In such a formal and nomenclatural fog, the Forward Prize judges – Annalena McAfee of *The Guardian*, Brian Patten the poet, Bill Swainson of Bloomsbury Publishing, myself and Jo Shapcott, winner of last year's Best Collection Prize with *My Life Asleep* – had their work cut out. We read everything, sent in our individual shortlists of five books of poems in each category, and met in Forward's Regent Street office at the beginning of July to try and synthesise our enthusiasms.

The result is this anthology, which, we believe, represents all that is best in modern British poetry. Arriving at the fifteen names in the final shortlists was an exciting, sometimes heated, process, as the judges argued, pooh-poohed each other's choices, recited favourite poems in hushed and theatrical voices, horse-traded, wept and strove to reach a consensus rather than a compromise. Poets who had failed to make the long lists were suddenly recalled from oblivion, hauled into the limelight and voted for. All the judges enjoyed the frisson of discovery which means you've encountered the real thing in a first collection, whether it was the Far Side gothic landscapes of Andrew Waterhouse, or the wry Jewish humour of Joanne Limburg. The Best Collection Prize drew the most robust discussion, but the virtues of John Burnside, Michael Donaghy, Douglas Dunn, Kathleen Jamie and Matthew Sweeney shone through.

The Forward Prize organisers provide a valuable service in the second half of this anthology, by letting the judges fill its pages with favourite poems whose authors didn't make the final cut. It's a pleasure to be able to feature such wayward talents as Roddy Lumsden, Stephen Dobyns, Polly Clark and Jeremy Reed along with more established names such as Thom Gunn, Michael Longley, Les Murray, Sharon Olds and Tom Paulin.

Whatever you expect from poetry – mind music, rinsed-out language, rhythmic excitement, wisdom, space age narratives, sacred mysteries – you'll find it here. And with any luck, you'll find something unexpected but equally rich on the next page. It's been a huge enterprise, judging a nation's poetic output on the cusp of the century, and the judges hope their lovingly fought-over selection will move and delight readers, whatever it is they want from poetry in their age.

John Walsh

Acknowledgements

Connie Bensley · GETTING OUT OF HAND · *The Back and the Front of It* ·
    Bloodaxe Books

Sujata Bhatt · GREEN AMBER IN RIGA · *Augatora* · Carcanet

Tessa Biddington · THE DEATH OF DESCARTES · The Bridport Prize

Colette Bryce · MY THEORY · PHONE · *The Heel of Bernadette* · Picador

John Burnside · DESSERTS · HUSBANDRY · *The Asylum Dance* · Cape Poetry

Polly Clark · THE FOOT-SOLDIER · *Kiss* · Bloodaxe Books

Tim Cumming · BREATHLESS · *Apocalypso* · Stride

Fred D'Aguiar · FROM BLOODLINES · *Bloodlines* · Chatto & Windus

Stephen Dobyns · THUS HE ENDURED · *Pallbearers Envying the One Who Rides* ·
    Bloodaxe Books

Michael Donaghy · CALIBAN'S BOOKS · MY FLU · *Conjure* · Picador

Douglas Dunn · FROM THE DONKEY'S EARS · *The Donkey's Ears* · Faber and Faber

Elaine Feinstein · IN PRAISE OF FLAIR · *Gold* · Carcanet

Catherine Fisher · EILMER OF MALMESBURY · *Altered States* · Seren

Matthew Francis · THE ORNAMENTAL HERMIT · Times Literary Supplement

Jane Griffiths · A POEM AGAINST THE KIND OF OCCASIONAL VERSE ·
    A Grip On Thin Air · Bloodaxe Books

Thom Gunn · SATURDAY NIGHT · *Boss Cupid* · Faber and Faber

Robert Hamberger · DIE BRAVELY · Acumen

John Heath-Stubbs · TEN KINDS OF BIRDS · *The Sound of Light* · Carcanet

Brian Henry · ARGONAUT SONATA · SKIN · *Astronaut* · Arc

Douglas Houston · PROVISIONAL · *The Welsh Book of the Dead* · Seren

Kathleen Jamie · FORGET IT · MEADOWSWEET · *Jizzen* · Picador

Alan Jenkins · THE ROAD LESS TRAVELLED · *The Drift* · Chatto & Windus

Dane Lavrnja · MOONTYPE · The Interpreter's House

Joanne Limburg · OUT WITH THE MUSE · THE WOULD-BES ·
    Femenismo · Bloodaxe Books

S J Litherland · A STORY ABOUT CRICKET · *The Apple Exchange* · Flambard

Michael Longley · THE WAR GRAVES · *The Weather in Japan* · Cape Poetry

Matthew Sweeney · Incident in Exeter Station · Sweeney ·
 A Smell of Fish · Cape Poetry
Andrew Waterhouse · Another Poem About the End of the World ·
 Looking for a Comet · *In* · The Rialto
C K Williams · Ice · *Repair* · Bloodaxe Books
Frances Williams · Oyster Eating · *Wild Blue* · Seren
Hugo Williams · Bar Italia · *Billy's Rain* · Faber and Faber
Cliff Yates · Clara · *Henry's Clock* · Smith/Doorstop Books

Contents

The Best Collection Poems

John Burnside

DESSERTS

and afterwards
    travelling home
on the northbound train
my body is wired
     to the flavours
of childhood:
    aniseed
and mint
   and something sharp
or incompletely sweetened
      like the stalks
of rhubarb we would cut from old
allotments
    dipped
in stolen sugar
    reddled at the lips
and trying to imagine nights like this:
a butterkist warmth on my tongue
      and the craquelure
of egg-yolk
   and cream of the well
on the maze of your skin.

HUSBANDRY

Why children make pulp of slugs
with a sprinkling of salt

or hang a nest of fledglings on a gate
with stolen pins

is why I sometimes turn towards the dark
and leave you guessing.

only to know the butter and nickel taste
of cruelty;
                to watch, and show no sign

of having seen
                    Not
wickedness, that sometimes celebrates

a tightness in the mind;
but what I comprehend

of fear and love:
cradled remoteness, nurtured by stalled desire;

willed deprivation;
the silence I'm learning by heart.

Michael Donaghy

CALIBAN'S BOOKS

Hair oil, boiled sweets, chalk dust, squid's ink...
Bear with me. I'm trying to conjure my father,
age fourteen, as Caliban – picked by Mr Quinn
for the role he was born to play because
'I was the handsomest boy at school'
he'll say, straight faced, at fifty.
This isn't easy. I've only half the spell,
and I won't be born for twenty years.
I'm trying for rainlight on Belfast Lough
and listening for a small, blunt accent
barking over the hiss of a stove getting louder like surf.
But how can I read when the schoolroom's gone
black as the hold of a ship? Start again.

Hair oil, boiled sweets...
But his paperbacks are crumbling in my hands,
seachanged bouquets, each brown page
scribbled on, underlined, memorized,
forgotten like used pornography:
The Pocket Treasury of English Verse
How to Win Friends and Influence People
Thirty Days To a More Powerful Vocabulary

Fish stink, pitch stink, seaspray, cedarwood...
I seem to have brought us to the port of Naples,
midnight, to a shadow below deck
dreaming of a distant island.
So many years, so many ports ago!
The moment comes. It slips from the hold
and knucklewalks across the dark piazza
sobbing *maestro! maestro!* But the duke's long dead
and all his magic books are drowned.

My Flu

I'd swear blind it's June, 1962.
Oswald's back from Minsk. U2s glide over Cuba.
My cousin's in Saigon. My father's in bed
with my mother. I'm eight and in bed with my flu.
I'd *swear*, but I can't be recalling this sharp reek of Vicks,
the bedroom's fevered wallpaper, the neighbour's TV,
the rain, the tyres' hiss through rain, the rain smell.
This would never stand up in court – I'm asleep.

I'm curled up, shivering, fighting to wake,
but I can't turn my face from the pit in the woods
– snow filling the broken suitcases, a boy curled up,
like me, as if asleep, except he has no eyes.
One of my father's stories from the war
has got behind my face and filmed itself:
the village written off the map, its only witnesses
marched to the trees. Now all the birds fly up at once.

And who filmed *this* for us, a boy asleep in 1962
his long-forgotten room, his flu, this endless rain,
the skewed fan rattling, the shouts next door?
My fever reaches 104. But suddenly he's here,
I'd swear, all round me, his hand beneath my head
until one world rings truer than the other.

Douglas Dunn

FROM THE DONKEY'S EARS (PART THREE, SECTION V)

Sea-holy rituals, crossing the Equator,
Neptune with trident and a flaxen beard,
A boy got up as Venus, brassièred
Boy-goddess, and the Symbolic Navigator. . .

Men watched the drama from the foreturret,
Perched on the crosstrees, on the yards and masts
In an exploded pyramid of castes –
An admiral, his officers, a water-butt

For democratic ducking, and no one saved
From the misrule, high-jinks and carnival.
'Good,' Ignatzius said. 'Good for men's morale' –
Facing an outsized razor, duly shaved.

Free for a day, each man a mutineer
Beyond the reach of law or etiquette
Other than Neptune's. Everyman gets wet
When crossing to the southern hemisphere.

Fictitious secrecy. Pamphlets and tracts
Discovered in the sweaty fo'c'sles prove
Rebellious limits to political love.
Crazed with the joyful mischief of our *Pax*

Equatoria, we could forget the seethe
Below-decks where the hidden policemen skulk
In every unofficial prison-hulk,
This fleet of fools, this dangerous air we breathe.

From The Donkey's Ears *(Part Six, Section I)*

You haunt my poem, the way a woman should
Inhabit her husband's verses. Yes, yes,
We've put to sea. Eastern geographies
Stretch before us, part-charted on the nude

Indian Ocean, miles and miles of tears
And sweat for me, and all my sweet devoirs
Directed at imagined moon and stars
Caught in a birch branch for a hundred years.

To find a glimpse of who I am, or what,
I'll have to swallow Russia and a sea.
Each verst of water looks the same to me,
Like walking on the steppes, from one named spot

To one named spot, to one named spot, the same
And endlessly the same, an onion-steepled
Toy landmark hinting that the place is peopled,
Though only those who live there say its name

Other than tax-collectors. Here, Ocean is
Uncharted, unpoliced. It's not a 'here',
Or place. It's a nowhere. It isn't fear
Forces me say this, this big notionless

Wonder that wet space should be so spacious
Now that no land's in sight, and I'm cut free
From earth again, let loose, and this vast sea
My element, an endlessly audacious

Physics and meditation for the eye
And soul. Not fear, but welcome to such space
And welcome, welcome, to the salt no-place
Where the unbirded winds intensify

Existence to the tip of an extreme
And any time it's silent its silence is
Sinister, sudden, unexpectedness
Dwarfing all senses, an unuttered scream.

Kathleen Jamie

FORGET IT

History in a new scheme. I stretch
through hip, ribs, oxter, bursting
the cuff of my school shirt, because
this, Mr Hanning, is me.
'Sir! Sir! Sir!
– he turns, and I claim
just one of these stories,
razed places, important as castles,
as my own. *Mum!*

We done the slums today!
I bawled from the glass
front door she'd long desired.
What for? bangs the oven shut,
Some history's better forgot.
              So how come
we remember the years
before we were born? Gutters
still pocked with fifties rain,
trains cruised dim
street-lit afternoons; war
at our backs. The black door
of the close wheezed
till you turned the third stair
then resounded like cannon.
A tower of bannisters. Nana
and me toiled past windows
smeared in blackout, condemned
empty stone. The neighbours had flitted
to council-schemes, or disappeared...

Who were the disappeared? Whose
the cut-throat

razor on the mantelpiece, what man's
coat hung thick with town gas, coal
in the lobby press?
                    And I mind
being stood, washed like a dog
with kettle and one cold tap
in a sink plumbed sheer
from the window
to the back midden
as multistoreys rose
across the goods yard,
and shunters clanked
through nights shared
in the kitchen recess bed.

*I dreamed about my sister in America
I doot she's dead.* What rural
feyness this? Another sibling
lost in Atlantic cloud,
a hint of sea in the rain –
the married in England,
the drunken and the mad,
a couple of notes postmarked Canada,
then mist: but this is a past
not yet done, else how come
our parents slam shut, deny
like criminals: *I can't remember, cannae
mind,* then turn at bay: *Why?*

Who wants to know? Stories
spoken through the mouths
of closes: who cares
who trudged those worn stairs,
or played in now rubbled back greens?
*What happened about my granddad? Why
did Agnes go? How come
you don't know*

that stories are balm,
ease their own pain, contain
a beginning, a middle –
and ours is a long driech
now-demolished street. *Forget it!*
Forget them that vanished,
voted with their feet,
away for good
or ill through the black door
even before the great clearance came,
turning tenements outside-in,
exposing gas pipes, hearths
in damaged gables, wallpaper
hanging limp and stained
in the shaming rain.

History, Mr Hanning.
The garden shrank for winter,
and mum stirred our spaghetti hoops
not long before she started back
part-time at Debenhams
to save for Christmas,
the odd wee
luxury, our first
foreign
holiday.

MEADOWSWEET

*Tradition suggests that certain of the Gaelic
women poets were buried face down.*

So they buried her, and turned home,
a drab psalm
hanging about them like haar,

not knowing the liquid
trickling from her lips
would seek its way down,

and that caught in her slowly
unravelling plait of grey hair
were summer seeds:

meadowsweet, bastard balm,
tokens of honesty, already
beginning their crawl

toward light, so showing her,
when the time came,
how to dig herself out –

to surface and greet them,
mouth young, and full again
of dirt, and spit, and poetry.

Matthew Sweeney

INCIDENT IN EXETER STATION
for Eddie Linden

He came in the door, staring at me,
like he'd known me in another life.
'I've chased everywhere after you,' he said.
'Years and years, I've been on the road,
too many to count. The train-fares,
the bus-fares, the plane-fares...
The least you can do is buy me a pint.'
He plonked his duffle-bag on the floor
and sat on the stool next to mine.
He looked in my eyes like a holy man,
said 'You're looking well, you've lost weight.'
His face could have done with flesh.
His hair needed a cut and a wash.
'I don't know you', I said, 'I've never,
ever seen you before.' He smiled,
the same smile Jesus must have flashed
at Judas, then his face changed
into a voodoo mask, as he shouted
'After all I've done for you!',
turning to face the roomful of eaters
and drinkers, all of whom ignored him
but I knew they classed us together,
so, seeing a train pull up at the platform,
I grabbed my hat, bags and ran,
getting in just as the train was leaving,
not knowing where it was headed,
hearing his roars follow me out
into the green Devon countryside
that I'd never risk visiting again.

Sweeney

Even when I said my head was shrinking
he didn't believe me. Change doctors, I thought,
but why bother? We're all hypochondriacs,
and those feathers pushing through my pores
were psychosomatic. My wife was the same
till I pecked her, trying to kiss her, one morning,
scratching her feet with my claws, cawing
good morning till she left the bed with a scream.

I moved out then, onto a branch of the oak
behind the house. That way I could see her
as she opened the car, on her way to work.
Being a crow didn't stop me fancying her,
especially when she wore that short black number
I'd bought her in Berlin. I don't know if she
noticed me. I never saw her look up.
I did see boxes of my books going out.

The nest was a problem. My wife had cursed me
for being useless at DIY, and it was no better now.
I wasn't a natural flier, either, so I sat
in that tree, soaking, shivering, all day.
Everytime I saw someone carrying a bottle of wine
I cawed. A takeaway curry was worse.
And the day I saw my wife come home
with a man, I flew finally into our wall.

The Best First Collection Poems

Colette Bryce

My Theory

I'm watching, Rat, as you shift about,
from my upstair opposite vantage point.
You happen, large and sudden,
in someone's scrap of garden.
Part obscured by the tinder litter,
swept and stirred by the winds all winter,
Rat, you've come to prove to me
your being, your proximity,
in case I disbelieve.

I'm watching still. You skulk and freeze.
A car approaches, enters, leaves
its roar in the road between us.
And you resume your snuffling,
examining and crumpling
discarded plastic bags.
Minutes slow and limp and drag.
I wait you out, determined now
to face the tail, the teeth, the claw,

you crawl across the balding grass
to streetlight stooped across the path
and there at last you're clear to me,
not quick and sleek and cheeky –
but a portly, lumberly, punk of a shape?
Ah Hedgehog, here like an act of grace,
tonight, with thanks to you,
my theory on the absence
of the objects of my fear holds true.

Phone

Though we've come to hate this line
we call; stuck evenings when we've dried
the well of talk, we bide the time
in small long-distance silences
and lend ourselves as audience
to voices washed from tense to tense
across the middle air.

So, often, more than I can bear,
missing you brings this desire
at least to hear and to be heard
and then, there's something to be said
for this. For this becomes a web,
becomes a hair, a strength, a thread,
a harness between us, in all fairness,
you in my hereness, me in your thereness.

Brian Henry

ARGONAUT SONATA

With no one to stop my launch into panegyric,
I take the warp and weft
in my hands with plans to commandeer this vessel
to a new hemisphere.

Of course, the vessel being sea wracked
and my atlas bereft
of any destination but the Wessel
Is., I'm sure to founder,

founder of nothing but one phonetic
and the occasional tuft,
tassel
or shock of hair

– cowlicked, no doubt – left
under a trestle, caught unaware.

§

Under a trestle, caught unaware, the vessel
– let's not call the raft
the raft – waxes poetic.
It goes nowhere.

Going nowhere fast, I part and parcel
my belongings onto the craft:
a nonpareil of patchwork.
I perch upon the chair

fastened like the watch to a castle,
wait to be upped and offed,
delivered – anorectic
without the mal de mer

or muscles sore from too much work – in swift
and dramatic fashion to Angleterre.

§

No: in frenetic fashion to the Gulf of Carpentaria. And quick.
A true wayfarer,
I see a map as a hassle.
Better to be adrift

and considered quixotic
than safe at harbour,
scissile
and scintillant, admiring one's handicraft.

But such journeys, especially the bound-to-be-historic,
must be an adventure.
They require a dismissal
of conventional statecraft,

a reluctance to pack-by-list or listlessly prepare,
a refusal to practise sensible thrift.

§

Refusing to practise sensible thrift, I nestle
some wine on board, some Camembert –
a bishop in his bishopric,
properly stuffed and starched and cuffed.

All this hustle and bustle,
all this hoopla and fanfare
– by no means narcissistic –
has attracted something of a crowd. Some seem miffed.

Miffed or not, they're muzzled,
mute in the face of such a dare-
devil who – in this vessel with aquatic
aspirations – sits, stern and abaft.

And the whistle – prepared for this affair,
its blast electric – sends me aloft –

Skin

Never mind the fantasy about the tweezers and the tongue,
the one about the bicycle pump and the twisted rim.
Never mind the angle of penetration, or the number
of blessed repetitions in the series of withdrawals and givings-in.

Never mind the dream about the bean-bag chair and the virgin,
the one about the tree and the bull terrier off its chain.
Never mind the song the words will not attach to,
the visions that arrive with the noises next door,

when a sneeze, or a sob, is mistaken for something else
and someone finds himself clinging to the wall,
perhaps with a glass to his ear, or his glasses on,
hoping something dark and old-fashioned has pulled him

from sleep this close to dawn. Never mind the crack
between the blinds and the sill, where a single moan
will keep him waiting an hour for another, his face pressed
against the pane, one eye open, half-blind but guided.

And never mind the woman in the grass beneath the statue.
Her palms are cupping her head, her skirt an inch off-centre,
glasses gleaming as the sun hums on the monument
of the general, the skin of her arms slowly going red.

Joanne Limburg

Out with the Muse

The Muse and I
are out on the piss.
He's squeezed up next to me,
with a bottle of Bud
and eyes that follow the barmaid.

He says he likes
a woman who can drink,
but I have to admit
I can't keep up with him –
he's several centuries ahead,
and I'm too slight a vessel
for his kind of inspiration.

I tell him I work in the morning.
'No.' he says, 'No.
You don't need that.
You and me, we're bohemians,
artists, we're above common values.
Have another.
Tell them you're sick.'

I am sick.
I take the last bus home
and fall through the front door,
reaching the bathroom just in time
to bow to Apollo
in his porcelain temple.

THE WOULD-BES

We're not yet human, but we're trying.
We're taking notes, we're taking classes.
We're taking medication. It can
take surgery to straighten kinks

as bad as ours. Sometimes it hurts –
you have to suffer to be human.
Sometimes we cry into our pillows,
but please don't make too much of that:

our tears don't count. We're not yet human
enough to satisfy the judges
that we're not just apes or dummies.
When they're sure they'll let us out

and then we'll live among the humans,
holding hands and pushing buggies,
drinking Coke, doing the things
everybody knows everybody does.

Owen Sheers

NOT YET MY MOTHER

Yesterday I found a photo
of you at seventeen,
holding a horse and smiling,
not yet my mother.

The tight riding hat hid your hair,
and your legs were still the long shins of a boy's.
You held the horse by the halter,
your hand a fist under its huge jaw.

The blown trees were still in the background
and the sky was grained by the old film stock,
but what caught me was your face,
which was mine.

And I thought, just for a second, that you were me.
But then I saw the woman's jacket,
nipped at the waist, the ballooned jodhpurs,
and of course the date, scratched in the corner.

All of which told me again,
that this was you at seventeen, holding a horse
and smiling, not yet my mother,
although I was clearly already your child.

Old Horse, New Tricks

The vet was careful
to place the barrel of his gun
right on the swirl of hair
in the centre of her forehead.

In the silence after the explosion
she was still for a second,
as if she would stand in death
as she had stood in sleep.

We watched, an audience expecting tricks,
and eventually she obliged,
succumbing to the slow fold of her fall
with a buckling of the crooked back legs

and a comedy sideways lean that went too far.
There was little symmetry in her collapse,
just the natural pattern of pain.
Even her tongue was out of order,

escaping from the side of her jaw,
and dipping to taste the earth below,
like a child, stealing a taste of the cake
before it is served.

Andrew Waterhouse

ANOTHER POEM ABOUT THE END OF THE WORLD

Birds refuse to sing, even at dawn, even for the cameras.
They return to last summer's nests tight-beaked, crouch.
Safe eggs form around them. In a black case my favourite
red butterfly is drinking its own wings, becomes molten.
The hare slowly blinks from its perfect hollow, looks away
as I pass. There are pollen clouds flowing through
half-dismantled webs, past the tree refolding its leaves;
flowing back to the grasses of the summer plain, that yellow,
withdraw roots, let the soil loose to dance.

Meanwhile, we sit in darkened rooms, make conversation,
watch our volunteers at work. They paint the river bed blue,
but the stones are hot, will never dry. They inflate clouds
and release them from hilltops. Also, my aunt has recycled
her second husband. Also, I buy a low energy personality,
but it is too late. The weather is quickening to a gale
blowing sand from continent to continent, filling our mouths,
our industrial estates. We fall gasping as the grains build up,
making dunes of us all by the risen ocean. And afterwards,
there may be something of a silence, a natural pause;
until the fresh rain, germination, inhuman celebration.

Looking for the Comet

You push back the sheet, leave me
naked and cooling in the night air.
You stand by the window,
by the yellow flowers in their blue vase
and there's moon on your face and shoulders.
"It's here," you say, but I'm pretending sleep,
and just watch you, watching the comet
moving off towards the sun and beyond.

A car passes. Headlights fill the window,
making new shadows, that rise, then fall.
You take a flower from the vase,
carry it to me in both hands, slowly wipe
the petals over my face. Now, I can smell
the pollen on my skin, feel the trail.

The Best Individual Poems

Tessa Biddington

THE DEATH OF DESCARTES

Fever clings to the bed like a rainforest.
Under its canopy a man mumbles his dream
to the servant and the doctor and the Comte,
who strain to hear beyond the wheezings
and whistlings of pneumonia. There is
nothing decipherable except:

Fleas! The Queen is at war! he shouts.
The doctor and the Comte and, behind them,
the servant each shake their heads.

The dream is a castle of cold stone and ice
where he is summoned to teach. He stands
in the cold stone library looking out at the ice,
his philosophy freezing to an ache in his bones.
The Queen has again excused herself on account
of matters of state and he hopes she is better
at ruling than grasping the principles of his Meditations.
Her Majesty lacks concentration and insight.
He is perplexed at the dull thud, thump and rumble
that continue hour after hour to leach through the ceiling.

The dream is faces smeared ochre by candleflame.
The dream is cool water on his ragged lips; in his arid throat.

He wonders how he is so hot in this tomb of a castle,
and why the doctor has travelled so far to see him – that *was*
the doctor? And the thud, thump and rumble drift in dust
to the library floor. Why should he need a doctor?
Look how he gallops up the steep stairs and down
the corridor, not breathless when he bursts in on the source
of the noise where Queen Christina is loading a four-inch cannon.

I hear, she says, the fashion in England is fur collars
to attract the filthy fleas away from the hair.
But this is more entertaining. See?
And has a lighted taper poised.

This small! A cannon *this* small! For fleas!
His feeble hands describe an impossibility. The doctor
and the Comte and the servant know, as they wait
for his final lucidity, that he would expect them
to question the existence of such things.

Robert Hamberger

DIE BRAVELY

'Why this would make a man a man of salt,
To use his eyes for garden water-pots,
Ay, and laying autumn's dust. I will die bravely,
Like a smug bridegroom.'
'King Lear' (Act 4 Sc 6)

Morning After

Last night we threw all the junk overboard:
chucked out summer photos and simple promises,
their noise fat stones hitting water.
Last night we climbed into our life-rafts
like separate beds.

This morning
the marriage is floating away from us.

If we stretch we can still touch its rudder
its soaked wood.
Our hands are full enough, steadying ourselves in the wake
where there's no sound of gulls, no sight of land,
only sea growing flatter between us in a new light.

Your First Words

"Can I say hello to you?" We were eighteen
first night away from home, and I said yes.
You thought I looked safe. How could you guess
in years to come I'd sometimes leave the room when

you were talking, annul you like that, how often
I'd stone you with silence. If I managed to impress
that night with quotes from Plath it didn't take us
long to learn no-one lives by poetry alone.
Pillow-talk on student grants. Two virgins touching
skin and histories. Speech ran
its thread down boulevards and cul-de-sacs, finding
all there is to know about one person.
Twenty years on I barely know you, but thanks for asking.
Go back to that night and I'd say yes again.

Separation Suite

They sit a chair apart,
move when the counsellor calls them
to a room where they're meant to relate.

Three fawn chairs and they talk about needs.
She's only starting to imagine hers,
can't begin to name them. He's written a list.

Next week he's back without her.
One voice slumped against magnolia woodchip:
his pain aria, his monotonous solo.

Looking At Wedding Photos

Who are these kids dressed as adults, thinking
they can throw a promise at the future
and it won't shatter after sixteen years? They're
sticking a knife in the cake hand over hand, grinning
fit to burst. Remember that Just Married sign
felt-tipped on the back of a Rat Poison container,

your dad getting lost, yellow roses, our
first married row on the wedding
night round Salisbury's one-way system. All gone.
What happened next? Happiness. Mistakes. Slowly seeing
we've
got to cut our losses. I won't burn
these smiles. They're proof of love,
while our children who never existed then
hold out their gifts: three reasons to survive.

The Old Words

While my hands soak up to their wrists in water
and the kids breathe asleep upstairs
my head's a hive with you and him naked in it.

Funny how the old words come back.
Fuck. Adultery. Cuckold. Betrayal.

I want this porn-film out of my hair:
to wash off what your body's doing, not doing
your skin a map I can no longer follow,
whetstone where a new knife twists.

Ivy House

A couple of dreamers. We'd make our ideal home.
So what if the owners were splitting up?
We were rock solid, seduced by each snowdrop
daffodil and door-frame, the view from every room.
We put down roots: damp-proofed, re-wired, sprayed
woodworm,
coated on buckets of gloss. We couldn't stop

until french windows had their cat-flap
and kids' hand-marks swiped the walls. It was high time
to look at what we'd done. I stayed tense
as barbed wire while you started scratching
a tunnel out. The builder said subsidence:
that quarter-inch crack down the north wall. Re-pointing
can't cure it. A fine romance.
It'll cost an arm and a leg now the drains are collapsing.

From Under The Shadow

Don't kid yourself it's easy.
My shadow's not as vacuous as air,
some sticky web wiped from footsoles.
It's heavy as a man's body on you
squeezing out your breath.

We pressed grids across each other
tattooing a street-plan of bruises
under our skin: husband father wife mother.
Live in my image. We couldn't fit.

Rip the maps,
learn our names again, recognize for the first time
your face, my face at noon where nettle paths divide
and our shadows shrink to puddles we step over.

Slow Learner

I keep rehearsing the call you won't make
one night near midnight in a few months: "I was wrong.
He's nothing to me. I've loved you all along.
I see things now. I made a mistake.

We both did, but we've learnt from it. If we take
our time maybe we could look at starting again." This daft song
round my skull, these phrases that don't belong
in your mouth but in mine, or that fake
image I still have of you. I never could see
what was an inch from my nose. It's like two days
before Clifford died, when they'd already
upped the morphine, his doctor friend says
"You know he's dying don't you?" I thought he can't be.
He'll recover. Pinning my hopes on another bad phase.

Talk Before Bedtime

Our son touches his forehead
runs a hand down his body to his feet:
"I felt sad from here to here."

We talk about sadness
how you and I can't make each other happy.

Squeezing my ribs in his tightest bear-hug
he laughs and asks "Does that hurt?"

In Front Of The Kids

When I cried in front of the kids they asked why.
"I've made you unhappy." That was enough.
I didn't add no-one would choose this rough
ride for their children, how I followed my
father's footsteps by walking out. That advert family
drops through the floorboards. I won't bluff
my way through failing as husband or father. My tough
son ran for toilet-paper to dry

my eyes. He said "I want to see you"
and gently held my face between his hands.
If this home's broken we'll build something new
from the four times a week when I'm with them, stroking
                                        strands
of hair off their hot brows. We slip through
absences, over stones, and our river never ends.

Benediction

Bless you for entering through a door-crack
and opening windows. For three children.
Without them my life would be one room,
books and a bare lightbulb, a locked cupboard.

For knowing when we needed to end:
saving us years of petty victories
over dinner, on a drive, our children
watching and hearing, a gagged audience.

For handing me back to myself:
giving up your responsibility, saying
"He's yours now. Make of his life what you can."

Truce

Call a truce. I'll bite my tongue and remember
how your breath fanned my back while we slept.
If it tickled my skin I shifted, slipped
an arm around your waist sometimes, or under
the duvet on good nights you squeezed my shoulder.
No need for talking in our sleep. Our bodies kept
their independent language, whose tides swept

us up pebbles and rolled us down. Until the past year
made us kneel yards apart on a hard coast.
Six weeks after we faced that truth
it was almost the old days. You dozed on my chest
as if you were my wife again, my breath
against your hair. Letting go. The last time we kissed
I lightly nipped your tongue between my teeth.

Her Voice

I haven't walked far enough. I can still hear it:
her words repeat in my head
until they're mine.

Hedges creak in the wind like bed-springs.
Her voice will go the way of rain:
shrink to a shallowing puddle, dry in the sun.

I can sit it out
while that noise from one skylark in the next field
flickers its singed coal above my breathing.

Ruth Padel

CASCAVEL

We want to see how gems get made in Rio.
How jewel-hunters of Brazil are feather-probing,
As we speak, the red-earth mines
And those shadow-dancing caves and mountain streams,
    Where mythic venom-pushers like the *fer de lance*
Are ambushing nine (at least) species of gold and emerald frog
From under fallen logs. How rotating knife-wheels,
Dusted with diamond, release the voodoo-shine

Of morganite from ruddy gobs of neo-slingshot.
How you tell a good one by comparing it to master stones
    Picked out by crystallographers. We want
Jewel-surgeons, droves of them, in action,
Making the perfect cut. 'Marquise', 'Brilliante', 'Classic Drop'.

Well – fine. We get the lot. An eyeful of Brazilian tourmaline
In pink, blue, yellow, green. Citrine, to see off nightmares.
Amethyst, keeping you sober whatever the alcohol
Consumed. Emeralds with veins like fern,
    The beaten silk and cyanide of peridot
In its hibernated state. The burn
Of rubies, ghost-pale chrysoprase. And diamonds everywhere
Like dandruff. But then we get fed through to Sales –

To Rosa Klebb, the torturer from early-mid James Bond,
Plus rows of senior citizens – couple who just rolled up, like us,
    To take a look, and found themselves in second honeymoon
                                                            pose
Facing banks of Tiger Eye and Sherry Beryl, that set you back
Three thousand. All the sparklers, stones men hack

From mountains, rank, grind, set in gold
And buy for women to wear. 'What do you want to see?'

What do you think? An amber wedding wreath? A kingsize bed
With platinum sheets? That matching pair
    Of sapphire watches trimmed
With custard-gold gold leaf?
We're fine, thanks, as we are.
Years, now, we've worn rings

We gave each other, since you turned up with
(You said) a leopardskin bra, and smuggled an opal
    On my finger, here, instead. 'You're interested
In opals?' She shimmies us three trays. 'An opal is
Like pumice – soft. The flicks of fire,

These points of pink, blue, yellow, green,
Are billions – look – of water drops.
The more there are, more colour in the stone,
The more expensive.' Please. What *are* we doing here
    When we could be in the forest, or a bar?
Getting into opal hierarchies, you spot the really rare
One. 'Is she open Saturday?' Jesus. You'll be asking next
For credit facilities or Euro-checks. I slither us out

To the jungle's tapestries, wagon wheels of umbrella-fern
Glowing and glancing with rain
    Plus a drum-roll blues from five
(At least) species of frog. Sheer night falls, instantly, Fritz,
Whom we blindly trust (or do we?), goes ahead across the
                                                    stream

And up the mountain path with two big sticks, poking
Every pile of leaves, every loose (but pitch-black) rock.
My canvas-and-Velcro sandals (wet, no socks) follow the steps
Of your Nike trainers. Hand in hand, Indian file,
    Eros and Psyche under the Telephone Tree
(Whose lianas are ready to brain us), my freezing fingers up
Your sleeve, we sing to warn the snakes we're here.
'Rose of Tralee'. 'Moon River'. Hours later, soaking, we reach

A blue-tiled hut. The guard mixes sugarcane-husk
Martinis. Doubles. We admire his wall-art –
    Posters of eight local species of *cascavel*
(A.k.a. rattlesnake), each
Of whose bite leaves seven hours to live. Back home in the
                                       hotel,

Your PowerBook glistering with ants, the desk-lamp throws
A floating amber fan from your head around the wall,
And Rio roars outside. Alone,
Dry, safe (amazingly), we're both at work
    Above loonily perfect Copacabana Beach
Where little boys, lime green and glitter-rose,
Play manic soccer in soft sapphire dusk
To an audience of rearing, floodlit, diamond surf.

Pascale Petit

The Strait-Jackets

I lay the suitcase on Father's bed
and unzip it slowly, gently.
Inside, packed in cloth strait-jackets
lie forty live hummingbirds
tied down in rows, each tiny head
cushioned on a swaddled body.
I feed them from a flask of sugar water,
inserting every bill into the pipette,
then unwind their bindings
so Father can see their changing colours
as they dart around his room.
They hover inches from his face
as if he's a flower, their humming
just audible above the oxygen recycler.
For the first time since I've arrived
he's breathing easily, the cannula
attached to his nostrils almost slips out.
I don't know how long we sit there
but when I next glance at his face
he's asleep, lights from their feathers
still playing on his eyelids and cheeks.
It takes me hours to catch them all
and wrap them in their strait-jackets.
I work quietly, he's in such
a deep sleep he doesn't wake once.

Charles Simic

Past-Lives Therapy

They explained to me the bloody bandages
On the floor in the maternity ward in Rochester, NY,
Cured the backache I acquired bowing to my old master,
Made me stop putting thumbtacks around my bed.

They showed me, instead, an officer on horseback,
Waving a sabre next to a burning house,
And a barefoot woman wearing only her slip,
Hissing after him and calling him Lucifer.

Then, I was a straw-headed boy in patched overalls.
Come dark, a chicken would roost in my hair.
Some even laid eggs while I strummed my banjo,
While my mother and father crossed themselves.

Next, I saw myself inside an abandoned gas station
Constructing a machine made up of a dentist's chair,
A store dummy, an electric hair-dryer, steak knives...
When a lady fainted seeing me in my underwear.

Some nights, however, they opened a hundred doors,
Always to a different room, and could not find me.
There was only a short squeak now and then,
As if a bird had been trapped out there in the dark.

The Other Poems

Connie Bensley

Getting Out of Hand

Experimenting with virtual reality
she calls up a good-sized house, and in it she pops
Rupert Brooke, who comes out of his study
muttering octosyllabics and twisting
his inky fingers through his famous hair.

Remembering his penchant for anguished passion
she summons Charlotte Brontë – but something goes wrong
and it is Branwell who turns up, though it doesn't seem
to matter, and he falls into conversation with Rupert
about the rail service to Lulworth Cove.

They settle down for tea, and here comes Jane Austen
handing round the bread and butter. Cup in hand,
she leafs through a volume of diaries
found on the coffee table. Her eyes widen
and she drops the book with a nervous glance

over her shoulder, but there is no sign
of the author, for Joe Orton (if on the premises)
is engaged elsewhere. More figures
materialise, and surely someone will have to wash
the cups – though that doesn't look like a butler

limping in through the French windows, saturnine
and patrician, with a dangerous-looking hound in tow.
Someone who understands these animals is needed a.s.a.p.
and Conan Doyle springs to mind – being also qualified
to advise about the foot – but no, surely that's GBS

cycling bossily up through the garden
ready to sort everyone out, if he can make himself heard
above the shouting and barking. Now they're all
comparing something, and fragments of speech surface:
Missolonghi . . . mosquito . . . my best apple tree.

Sujata Bhatt

GREEN AMBER IN RIGA
for Gunnar Cirulis

The woman on the street corner
was selling necklaces
    made of green amber.

Soon everywhere we turned
someone was selling amber:
necklaces, bracelets, nuggets with insects
                  trapped inside –
But it was the green amber
that seemed closest to the sea,
as if it had just been pulled
        out yesterday –

It was the raw texture
      of the green amber
I thought of, Gunnar,
as we sat in your house
and you poured the sap from birch trees
      into our glasses –

You pointed out the window
your uncle liked to look out of –
the room your father used
    to work in.
'This was our home – this was
our home. . .' you kept on
repeating with such joy –
your feet emphatic on the floor.

Your family home
taken over by the Red Army
and used for so long
as officers' living quarters –
Your family home suddenly
returned to you, empty –
your childhood returned to you
        in your old age.

Polly Clark

THE FOOT-SOLDIER

As though I would survive,
I forgave the digging of my body
in preparation for war.
I had my basic training,

I clutched my rations to me
and counted them at night.
At dawn I pushed aside the corpses
and went over the top.

I stumbled through no man's land,
living miracle after miracle,
that I could still hurt, that I still lived,
that I might reach the other side.

They gave me a badge and an office
and I ignored the devastation,
the bodies upright as though neatly shot,
the corpses guzzling in their suits,

the long corridors all leading to loss,
the empty screens crackling against my fingers.
As though I would survive
I *became good*, I *learned to love*.

At night I curled and dreamed
I was alive. By day I neatly filed
my names away, ticking as appropriate
squandered, stolen, marched away at gunpoint.

Tim Cumming

BREATHLESS

Suddenly he'd walk breathless into a room
or catch his breath on stairs,
at dawn, when a phone would ring,
and his heart would skip a beat.
He'd catch his clothing, or lose the key,
the plot, the sense of anything
having a recognisable purpose.
He once read a book about relaxation
and even bought a cassette
and when he slept his visions
were like the label on a bottle of good wine.
Sleep, breathlessness, and a temporary
inability to take things seriously.
The sense of having too much of everything on one plate
and the attention span of a bird's wing.
A bird caught in a smallish room.
He sat alone in his room
and hugged the phone to his chest,
counting the pips first to one hour,
and then the next.

Fred D'Aguiar

Stella remembered the moment she died
as a woman and person and the shell
of the rest of her days took over her insides.
She was nine or ten, she wasn't sure, you couldn't tell,
carrying a message for her master with pride
but with a child's bearing and on a child's stroll.
At the crossroads she saw a man in a cage
hoisted from a tree, barely a man's age;

a battalion of flies; a mass of bones and flesh;
a gauze woven an acre wide of the particular
stench of clotted blood, and that blood in a nest
at the foot of the cage, drop by peculiar
drop falling in strings, adding to the mess
underneath, each string breaking to form another.
She screamed, turned and ran, not glancing back,
feeling that cage gaining on her back.

Her sweat became that blood, the man's skin
her skin. She fought for each shallow breath.
Somehow she'd caught the dead man's stink.
She swallowed air but tasted blood and death.
She scrubbed herself; refused food and drink.
When questioned she tried but couldn't speak.
Rescued from scrubbing, she only ate
soap and went four days straight awake.

They pinned her and forced food down,
mixed with bush tea doubling as sleep medicine,
boiled by them into a deep-green alluvium,

burying any leftovers of that nameless, certain
plant, coveted and antediluvian,
spoken about in hushed tones, unwritten.
It made her sleep but her eyes refused to close;
still seeing the cage with that man in no clothes.

She's no longer a girl or an African.
She died on her feet, propelled by rage.
She fled her body as only the free can.
Asleep, she replaces him in his cage
at the crossroads. Her body's all broken,
an oil-slick of her blood mirrors her visage,
there for all to see what becomes of the slave
who tries to rise above the station of the trade.

Stephen Dobyns

Thus He Endured

Heart's friend Greasy gets nixed by a stroke.
His pals give him a wake; they drink all night.
The next day they cart the coffin to the church.
In life, Greasy waxed cars; now he's defunct.
The priest says how Greasy's in a better place.
Heart takes exception. What could beat this?
Some mourners weep; others scratch their butts.
In life, Greasy was a practical joker. Even salt
in the sugar bowl wasn't too childish for him.
When the service is over, Heart and five friends
heave the coffin on top of their shoulders.
Outside it's raining. They wait for the hearse.
Maybe it's late, maybe it showed up and left.
The priest locks the church. The last cars depart.
Let's carry the coffin, it's just a few blocks.
As they set off, Heart hears a whistle. Show some
respect, he complains to a buddy in back.
In life, Greasy often asked, What's the point
and What comes next? Heart thought his jokes
helped keep the dark at arm's length. Rain drips
down the pallbearers' necks. Because of the fog
they can't see beyond their noses. Right or left?
If their hands weren't full, they would flip a coin.
Someone plays the harmonica, then starts to sing.
The pallbearers look at each other, it's none of them.
In life, Greasy reached three score years and ten.
He had a wife, four sons, and five Great Danes,
but not all at once. He always drove a Chevrolet.
Did we take a wrong turn? asks Heart. The rain
turns to sleet; it's getting dark. Someone starts
playing the trombone. A tune both melancholy
and upbeat. Where could it be coming from?
In life, Greasy felt a lack. He worked too hard,

the holidays were short. His wife kept asking
why he didn't do better. Then his sons left home.
Greasy stuck rubber dog messes on the hoods
of his friends' cars. This is what life's all about,
he'd think. Thus he endured. It begins to snow.
Heart shoulders his load. The sun goes down.
Will Greasy get planted today? It looks unlikely.
Heart watches the road. He can't see that the coffin lid
is tilted up and Greasy perches on top, just a shadow
of his former self. With both hands he flings wads
of confetti. He's a skeleton already. Heart would
scratch his head but he'd hate to let his corner drop,
his pals ditto: pallbearers envying the one who rides.

Elaine Feinstein

In Praise of Flair

That whole wet summer, I listened to Louis Armstrong.
Imagined him arriving in New York after Funky Butt
dance halls, wearing hick clothes: those
high top shoes with hooks, and long
underwear down to his socks.

Thought of him shy in a slick, new band, locked
for two weeks reading the part he was set,
until the night when Bailey on clarinet
took over an old song. Then Louis' horn
rose in harsh, elated notes,

of phrases he'd invented on riverboats
and ratty blues tonks, using all the sinews
of his face and muscle of his tongue.
And what delights me now,
is when he grinned to thank

the crowd that stood to clap, and saw
slyly from the corner of his eye
all the stingy players in the band
were sitting motionless, their tribute
only an astonished sigh.

Catherine Fisher

The books had crazed me. I gathered feathers,
goose and swan, down of sparrows
snagged on hedges. Some of each,
magpie and crow; I was thief and scavenger and hawk,
renewing my zig-zag vigour like an eagle.
      Barbs and flights, I preened them,
laid them on wicker frames, fixed with
pitch the quills I would write with now,
on the air, on history; and I climbed the
early morning to its top, up the body's stairs,
hearing far below my heart
pound on its locked door.

High, giddy, I looked out
from fear. Woods and roofs and tiny people
hung from my feet. The sky waited,
its arms wide open, feathered edges rippling.

And I remember, I still strain to keep, that slow
falling outward into joy, the air holding me
as I lay on it, the second of lifting when I knew
all truths, pierced all dreams, screamed
the raw hawk's rage, the sparrow's terror.
      Then collapse. Tumbled, buffeted down
the stones of the wall, rib to rib; the crumpling
smash of blackness that was earth.

I lived. Not as I used to live.
I had been Icarus, Bladud, all who trusted,
launched themselves out of sanity. Daily
I plummet back into that flight,
knowing what birds and angels know,
falling through God's fingers, endlessly.

Matthew Francis

THE ORNAMENTAL HERMIT

Not really ornamental, a white figure
you might glimpse from the drive, deep in the beech woods,
as you were making your way towards the house,
standing so still he might have been a long strip
of sunlight on the bark, except that you felt,
not his eyes on you exactly, but his *thoughts*.

Hardly anyone saw him close up. The cook,
who had, said he was wearing a floppy robe
of coarse stuff and looked like a man in a bag,
and a visitor who had come face to face
with what appeared to be a nightgowned person
supposed he was mad or walking in his sleep.

No one could agree on his age. The footman
who left last night's jellied fowl and potatoes
beside his sandbank grotto in the morning
would say, after a long pause, he thought the chap
wore spectacles but he stayed in the shadows
hunched over his Bible. They were not to speak.

He was a lover who had renounced the world
or else he had been promised a thousand pounds
if he could live for seven years in the cave
that had been scooped out for him, rising at dawn,
then brooding the whole day over the hourglass,
at night praying or reading by candlelight.

Hermits were all the rage these days but this one
could not have been laid on as an ornament
for houseparties. Some of the guests went so far
as to doubt his existence, or at least claimed
that he had long ago climbed the wall, leaving
his implements in the slowly filling hole.

But it was like this. There are times when a man
must grasp where he is living. It's not enough
any more to lie under your roof at night
hearing the dry rain, to own all those acres
of dark and dirt, without someone to feel it,
to be in the thick. That's what I paid him for.

Jane Griffiths

A Poem Against the Kind of Occasional Verse

which starts with a long quavering line like the run-up
to a marginal doodle on a set of lecture notes, the sort
which starts as a circle, becomes an eye, grows a quiff
and some flowers which sprout from an enormous ear
that's attached to a retrospective tea-pot spout
and culminates in a set of legs like those which belong
to an occasional table of the unassuming kind which
can always be pushed (almost) to one side: not just because
it's a way of playing consequences single-handed so even
the element of surprise is lost or because the ends of lines loiter
without intent like drunks on the pavement at closing-time but
mainly because of the pretence that the writer is simply
part of the scenery, part of a bar-stool or a swift triangle
of red skirt round the ellipse of the Sheldonian who has stumbled
upon herself as upon the occasional table or chair leg
and observed herself and written her down, unassuming
and pi as the artless voice on the telephone whispering
it's only me when really *it is I* all the time.

Thom Gunn

Saturday Night

I prowl the labyrinthine corridors
   And have a sense of being underground
As in a mine... dim light, the many floors,
   The bays, the heat, the tape's explosive sound.
People still entering, though it is 3 a.m.,
   Stripping at lockers and, with a towel tied round,
Stepping out hot for love or stratagem,
   Pausing at thresholds (wonder never ends),
Peering at others, as others peer at them
   Like people in shelters searching for their friends
Among the group come newest from the street.
   And in each room a different scene attends:
Friends by the bedful, lounging on one sheet,
   Playing cards, smoking, while the drugs come on,
Or watching the foot-traffic on the beat,
   Ready for every fresh phenomenon.
This was the Barracks, this the divine rage
   In 1975, that time is gone.
All here, of any looks, of any age,
   Will get whatever they are looking for,
Or something close, the rapture they engage
   Renewable each night.
                  If, furthermore,
Our Dionysian experiment
   To build a city never dared before
Dies without reaching to its full extent,
   At least in the endeavor we translate
Our common ecstasy to a brief ascent
   Of the complete, grasped, paradisal state
Against the wisdom pointing us away.

What hopeless hopefulness. I watch, I wait –
The embraces slip, and nothing seems to stay
   In our community of the carnal heart.
Some lose conviction in mid-arc of play,
   Their skin turns numb, they dress and will depart:
The perfect body, lingering on goodbyes,
   Cannot find strength now for another start.
Dealers move in, and murmuring advertise
   Drugs from each doorway with a business frown.
Mattresses lose their springs. Beds crack, capsize,
   And spill their occupants on the floor to drown.
Walls darken with the mold, or is it rash?
   At length the baths catch fire and then burn down,
And blackened beams dam up the bays of ash.

John Heath-Stubbs

TEN KINDS OF BIRDS
for John Minihan

Ten different kinds of birds I have identified
By their calls and songs as we sit here
Under a darkening sky of June, drinking our wine.
It was the wheezing call of the greenfinch
Greeted me on my arrival;
The robin redbreast, that sang to us
All the long Winter through, is hardly trying now –
I guess his brood is fledged and flown; from a fruit-tree
      near the house
The unpretentious song
Of the garden-warbler comes; the sparrow
Has only got one note, but he's working on it.
More eloquent the blackbird – there are two blackbirds
With adjoining territories – one answers
But not identically, the other's phrases –
Sweet and rich their songs. More shrill, more passionate,
A little way off, a thrush is singing also;
Farther still, perhaps at a copse's edge,
The foolish croodling of the wood-pigeon.

From the church tower, from time to time,
A party of jackdaws flies. They cruise round for a bit,
And then return. They talk to each other,
As is their custom: 'Let's keep together boys –
If there should happen to be a hawk around
She'd likely pick off a straggler.'
Now the not quite English accents
Of the collared dove sound somewhere to the right.
It seems he woke a chaffinch up,
Who then repeated his rattling tattle,
Ending with a phrase that sounds like 'ginger beer'
And then fell silent. So it goes on and on

Till one by one sleep claims the birds
As it must soon claim us. As we go in
There is a last blackbird. With sombre plumes
And golden mouth, he flings his melody
Into the darkness –
So let it be with me, when the night comes.

Douglas Houston

PROVISIONAL

What-is-the-case slips through the net of speech,
Something to do with missing you, the blues
Elaborating silence, out of reach

Of any lesson circumstance might teach.
The props are old harmonicas and booze.
What-is-the-case slips through the net of speech.

It was the same out walking on the beach,
The light upon the sea and other clues
Elaborating silence, out of reach,

Our distance, our disjunction each from each,
Our bondage to the styles we think we choose.
What-is-the-case slips through the net of speech,

Renews its half-life after every breach,
Love's not the sort of thing you want to lose.
Elaborating silence, out of reach,

It would not do to use the word "beseech",
Unless you're going to tighten all the screws;
What-is-the-case slips through the net of speech,
Elaborating silence, out of reach.

Alan Jenkins

THE ROAD LESS TRAVELLED

I've never scaled the heights of Machu Picchu with a backpack
or trekked through India, breakfasting on hunger,
or listened in the African night to the insects' claptrap,
smoked a peace-pipe on Big Sur, or surfed Down Under.

I never featured on the cork board in your kitchen
among the postcards from the friends who'd gone to Goa,
Guatemala, Guam; among the glossy shots of lichen-
and liana-festooned temples, girls who grin *Aloa!*

I never wrote, 'I have walked the sands of Dar-es-Salaam
and seen elephants drink from the great Zambezi';
'Moving on to Bogota'; 'Babar says *Salaam*
from San Francisco'; 'Here in Maui the living's easy'.

(I always sent my greetings from a *caffe, camera* or *chambre*
with a view of the Rose Window, Bridge of Sighs, Alhambra . . .)

But if I stand on my roof-top in London, West Eleven
with my head in the clouds of Cloudesley Place, North One
I can get it clear: how one day you'll move earth and heaven
to have me here, but I'll have changed tack, I'll be gone

in search of some more fascinating place or person,
I'll have made a fresh start, with no thought, now, of failure,
it won't be my emotions that you play on (or rehearse on),
it won't be my tongue that tastes the coastline of Australia

in the birthmark on your thigh; it won't be me who brings you
tea in bed, or a cappuccino with the froth still on it,
or performs my 'Dance to Morning' for you, or sings you
'The Shadow of your Smile', or writes a double sonnet

to you, to your freckled breasts, your sturdy
dancer's legs and neat behind (or, if that's too wordy

for your answering machine, ghazals
to your eyes that are the colour of the clear green water
of Sardinia), or puts on 'El cant dels ocells' by Casals
and holds the phone up to the speaker, or holds your daughter
to the sunrise in a suburban garden with galahs
and kookaburras, holds her up as if I'd caught her
to hear the song of the Catalan birds, and Bala's.

Dane Lavrnja

MOONTYPE*

A thought: That until Buzz steps down onto this ball of rock
Mine are the only footprints on this extraterrestrial beach.

My breath walks with me, side-by-side, yet static, trapped inside.
Until Buzz steps down mine are the only thoughts,

Mine is the only language, loss or gain, psychology, pain;
I have a monopoly of soul. I singularly represent the whole.

So when eventually I return, I can claim to be the man
Who did it first, who raked over the fine particles of the
     universe.

But back to this ball of rock. Behind my thumb the Earth
     disappears.
As if I flick a switch, removing it from the night, dousing
     sunlight.

I press it like a pin into the board of darkness, then another, and
     another.
Until each planet holds the message of the heavens.

Another thought: That even through the fabric of my temperate
     glove,
I will feel the braille of humanity ill at ease, drowning in its seven
     seas.

* *system of writing and printing for the blind*

S J Litherland

A STORY ABOUT CRICKET

I'm sure Hera looked down from Olympus
and spotted someone like you. (I'm sure
she did.) Bored with your work, herding

a few goats and sheep, taking time out
to play the lyre and sing. And she came
down to offer celestial conversation,

watching as you talked: your slim build,
bare arms, still hands, one wrist braceleted
with a woven rainbow thread, the single

ring on your finger; discovered your humour
defending yourself with deft strokes
flourished like a Gower of those times,

before the game was shaped from mood
and movement; you, displaying fair curls
like his as you talk, curls she hadn't

noticed until you touched them, your fair
beard hiding your youth, blue eyes hiding
your intensity most of the time.

Hera couldn't force you like Zeus
or seduce you like Aphrodite,
dreamt instead of her immortal soul

snaking into yours as you conversed.
That's what she dreamt. I know she did.
Powerless to touch you or your mind,

the man behind the mind, desiring the soul
inside the man where you are both equal.
This is a most conventional story.

Actually, you spotted her unaware,
noticed her inability to see you,
her naked face innocent of coquetry.

Hera caught in a moment of neglect.
You were the one watching who threw
a question, eyes sharp with attention

she suddenly saw and faltered at.
The Fates had delivered to her door
a beautiful young man. She couldn't

believe her luck except he was mortal.
Hera talked to her not-yet-cricketing
shepherd, dreamt of desire like a snake-

clasp coupling, desire where poetry
and music meet and hold fast, where
seamlessly we change into each other

leaving ourselves on the outside like clothes.
But don't think I'm Hera. This is only
a story about the beginning of cricket.

How it started as an art of conversation,
a wish of seduction, a compromise
of attraction, a sport they think

began among shepherds by a wicket gate
without the intervention of the goddess.
After five days Hera devised a game

in your image, of courtly strategy
and attack, tactics and defence,
above all, of fair play and deference

to a question of judgement, where
her soul and yours are the players
held together and apart by the rules.

Michael Longley

THE WAR GRAVES

The exhausted cathedral reaches nowhere near the sky
As though behind its buttresses wounded angels
Snooze in a halfway house of gargoyles, rainwater
By the mouthful, broken wings among pigeons' wings.

There will be no end to clearing up after the war
And only an imaginary harvest-home where once
The Germans drilled holes for dynamite, for fieldmice
To smuggle seeds and sow them inside these columns.

The headstones wipe out the horizon like a blizzard
And we can see no farther than the day they died,
As though all of them died together on the same day
And the war was that single momentous explosion.

Mothers and widows pruned these roses yesterday,
It seems, planted sweet william and mowed the lawn
After consultations with the dead, heads meeting
Over this year's seed catalogues and packets of seeds.

Around the shell holes not one poppy has appeared,
No symbolic flora, only the tiny whitish flowers
No one remembers the names of in time, brookweed
And fairy flax, say, lamb's lettuce and penny-cress.

In mine craters so vast they are called after cities
Violets thrive, as though strewn by each cataclysm
To sweeten the atmosphere and conceal death's smell
With a perfume that vanishes as soon as it is found.

At the Canadian front line permanent sandbags
And duckboards admit us to the underworld, and then
With the beavers we surface for long enough to hear
The huge lamentations of the wounded caribou.

Old pals in the visitors' book at Railway Hollow
Have scribbled 'The severest spot. The lads did well'
'We came to remember', and the woodpigeons too
Call from the wood and all the way from Accrington.

I don't know how Rifleman Parfitt, Corporal Vance,
Private Costello of the Duke of Wellingtons,
Driver Chapman, Topping, Atkinson, Duckworth,
Dorrell, Wood come to be written in my diary.

For as high as we can reach we touch-read the names
Of the disappeared, and shut our eyes and listen to
Finches' chitters and a blackbird's apprehensive cry
Accompanying Charles Sorley's monumental sonnet.

We describe the comet at Edward Thomas's grave
And, because he was a fisherman, that headlong
Motionless deflection looks like a fisherman's fly,
Two or three white after-feathers overlapping.

Geese on sentry duty, lambs, a clattering freight train
And a village graveyard encompass Wilfred Owen's
Allotment, and there we pick from a nettle bed
One celandine each, the flower that outwits winter.

Roddy Lumsden

IN THE WEDDING MUSEUM

This is why we're here and why we've swapped
admission money for these crimson ticket stubs
the guide has torn in two. The simple hall
is kept at constant temperature; four walls
of exhibition cases, glass and oak, are lined
with printed cards. Let's take a look around.
Two jars of morning air, lids sealed with lead.
A linen sheet which graced the marriage bed.
And here's a corkboard pinned with lists of guests,
last-minute shopping lines, musicians' sets,
the florists' chit. That bar-till roll is bull's-neck thick!
This bucket's where I-can't-remember-who was sick.
The marquee poles are here and champagne flutes
are poking from each pocket of the bridegroom's suit.
The sleeping bags of those who roughed it overnight.
A burst guitar string, coiled like an ammonite.
A wishbone which, for once, split half and half.
A dozen albums filled with photographs.
The bridegroom's tie, the best man's speech, the banns,
some skewers from the barbecue, some cups and cans
and candles. Here's a freeze-dried slice of wedding cake.
And here's the dress itself, still crisp and vacuum-packed.
This clod of soil's that very billionth part of Fife
where man and woman changed to husband, wife,
a decade back. And this is why we've come
to visit this museum, ten years on,
with these two children, blushing ear to ear,
who're laughing, knowing this is why they're here.

William Martin

SHARD
Version of an old Irish poem

Here is a song
That stags give tongue
In winter snows
After summer goes

High fell winds blow
When the sun is low
Its brief day song
In sea tossed throng

Bracken clumps hide
Red under white
Geese rise up
With accustomed cries

Cold encircles
Massed wings of birds
In the icy time
Bitter season's rhyme

Robert Minhinnick

VOICES FROM THE MUSEUM OF THE MOTHER OF ALL WARS

The Doorkeeper

>   Such a key!
Its lock a labyrinth
Of wards. Not even the daylight
Filters in.
>   How is it then
That the uranium
Dances through?

The Nurse

All my babies shrunken
    Like lemons in a bowl.

The Matchseller

Glance up.
>   Rigel.
>   Bellatrix.
>   Alpheratz.
Lit by a man in rags.

The Cleaner

The cruise missile
Is constructed from a cardboard packing case.

Standing alone in a dusty room
I cup its muzzle

And remember the riverbank near Karbala
Where I fed figs to a horse.

The Artist

I roll the clay between my palms.
    And look – a miracle.
The child is dancing naked before us.
Now on my brush her blood begins to gleam.

The Philosopher

        Listen. There is one lesson.
    If you would gather dates
Then you must wait beneath the palm.

The Stone Mason

Before the sun burns my neck
Arak will dry my throat.
            Blood of Allah.
One drop,
            two,
My sweat on the slab.
One drop, two, and the bottle
    Back under the jalabiyah.

The Beggar

You ask, what is the colour of thirst?
It starts green. And turns gold. And soon, I tell you,
It is redder than the red of the watermelon.

The Engineer

Come with me down one hundred steps
To where the pumps are stilled.

Welcome to the underworld!
And a lake such as you have never seen before.

But why turn away?
Why cover your mouth

As if you choked on a bone,
Or stopped yourself from crying out?

The Muezzin

Soldiers who spoke
A terrible language
Broke into the mosque.
Look, here are the words they wrote
In the blood of the boy who serves the priest.
Our translator weeps.

The Taxi Driver

They gave me all I asked
And a pepsi I will take home for my wife.
But see how, parked two hours under the palms,
The oil squeezes itself into the light.

The Guard

A woman brings me bread and dates.
I give her toilet paper.
So we stand under the green star and listen
To the night's first sirens,
To the muezzin through his microphone.
Then, slowly, faint as reeds in the Tigris,
Starts our own murmuring.

The Nun

They dug in the tombs
And found only lily roots.

Would they peer into the blue mouths of goats
Thinking them gun barrels?

The Teacher

Not a page, not a book, not a crayon.
If there was glass in the window
I would tell my children to breathe a mist
And with their forefingers write what has occurred.

The Curator

You have been the first visitors
For many days

So especially for you
I will open the secret room.

Could you have ever imagined
What lay within?

And thank you, thank you
For the big, grey 250 dinar notes

That you have plucked out like dead flowers.
Or the pages of a burnt book.

John Mole

SIMPLETON

They stopped him on his way to the fair
and asked impossible questions.
I don't know he answered, one by one,
but with a simple grin they might
find fetching. Not a bit of it. Their laughter
thundered overhead, a dark cloud
gathering impatience. Then there rained
such blows on him he knew for sure
he'd never get there. *We could tell you
everything*, they said, *but this is better
and was worth the wait*. At that
he lay face down and took it, weeping
earthwards. One by one
the stars came out, and then the moon
was there, by now too late
for anything but shining vacantly
on all of them. The road ahead
returned a distant music and the pulse
of love until whatever started this
was over. *Now if he doesn't know*
he heard them say, *he'll never*, as they
left him, as he rose and stood there
shrouded in the certainty of pain,
remembering the questions. Then
towards him, innocently decked
with ribbons from the fair, a girl
came dancing and she broke his heart.

David Morley

The Wakes

On the blue, four and two.
On the white, your camera-light.
Blackpool queues, how do you do's.
Blackpool's wealth, the brain's on a shelf.
Knock it back. Bring it up.

Glasgow Wake. Run on the clubs.
The zoo on Sunday, its all-hour pub.
The girls of wire, their tiny men,
the kiss, the rub, the bye bye hymen.
Gold rushed in from the offshore rigs.
The black stuff, cash; the men, the cogs.
Barnsley Wake. The smuts of air,
the skinned-up blow, the Solacare.
Downwind of the weather cock –
Heysham trawlers, Fleetwood Macs,
the Cod War punching at their backs.
The Cod War, the coldest war.
Welsh Wake. The train's a throat
boozing through Preston, cacking through Kirkham,
spuming in the forth of Blackpool North.
The cut-throat cabs, the pugs, the blabs,
the shot up cases, the bastard scabs.
Blackpool queues, the threats, the bruise.
Miner's Wake. Had it good,
then Miners' Strike; Cortonwood.
The Miners' strike, then the English knife.
A policemen's lot: nasty, short.
Blackpool taunts, how do you don'ts.
Blackpool's wealth, the brain's on a shelf.
Irish Wake. Gypsy-speak –
Irish Stew in the name of the bore.
God rushed in to the Belfast yards,

an Irish Card, a prod old guard.
Then the dollar's breath, a year-long death;
a boom, a bust. The shipyard's rust.
Rochdale Wake. Drink till you choke.
Knock it back, dog it up.
Knock her up. Kiss her quick.
Dog her quick. Knock her back.
The North Pier and tackled up.
A haul of fish, the flask. The mug.

Clickety-click, full house, drop-kick.
Blackpool queues, how do you do's.
Blackpool's wealth, the brain's on a shelf.
On the blue, four and two.
On the white, your camera-light.

Les Murray

MUSIC TO ME IS LIKE DAYS

Once played to attentive faces
music has broken its frame
its bodice of always-weak laces
the entirely promiscuous art
pours out in public spaces
accompanying everything, the selections
of sex and war, the rejections.
To jeans-wearers in zipped sporrans
it transmits an ideal body
continuously as theirs age. Warrens
of plastic tiles and mesh throats
dispense this aural money
this sleek accountancy of notes
deep feeling adrift from its feelers
thought that means everything at once
like a shrugging of cream shoulders
like paintings hung on park mesh
sonore doom soneer illy chesh
they lost the off switch in my lifetime
the world reverberates with Muzak
and Prozac. As it doesn't with poe-zac
(I did meet a Miss Universe named Verstak).
Music to me is like days
I rarely catch who composed them
if one's sublime I think God
my life-signs suspend. I nod
it's like both Stilton and cure
from one harpsichord-hum:
penicillium –
then I miss the Köchel number.
I scarcely know whose performance
of a limpid autumn noon is superior

I gather timbre outranks rhumba.
I often can't tell days apart
they are the consumers, not me
in my head collectables decay
I've half-heard every piece of music
the glorious big one with voice
the gleaming instrumental one, so choice
the hypnotic one like weed-smoke at a party
and the muscular one out of farty
cars that goes Whudda Whudda
Whudda like the compound oil heart
of a warrior not of this planet.

Helena Nelson

I
Mr Philpott, sitting naked in the conservatory,
examines the clouds descending on Ben Tee
in a distant squall. The sun sips at his skin
urging an instant pinkness. Mrs Philpott
(she is his second wife; he calls her 'dear')
bears in the morning beverage on a tray.
She is wearing a fresh apron, frilled with coy
rosebuds. Her lips open, enjoining him
to put on the Welsh Male Choirs – put them on *loud*.
Her wish is his command. Removing his glasses, he
flicks a switch which swells men's voices into
exultation, flooding the world with a surge
of joy. Outside the rain descends in sheets;
inside, the milk discreetly cools the tea.

II
On holiday without her children, Mrs Philpott
paints her nails and waits for them to dry.
Mr Philpott has gone up the burn with his rod
and his waders. What are they doing now,
her distant, grown-up babies? Taller than her
and wiser, they have told her there's no use
regretting the past: the prams, the pushchairs;
things, they say, move on, as people must – and she
should settle down, be positive, face it.
Therefore, each week she lets herself unfold
a little curve of fat. 'Voluptuous',
as Mr Philpott calls it. Do you think, he says,
we're in love? I want only you, she replies, and sighs.
Truth approaches. She does not embrace it.

III

In the conservatory, Mr Philpott waits in the dark
with only the moon for company. They have had a row,
he and she, a marital discordancy, a jangling of nerves.
Outside, the hills' grey curves and silvered thighs
swell into softness, rain slipping slow and steady
as heartbeats. Inside the silence swells and forms
a statement: absence of love, absence of love.
He absorbs the repetition, hearing her move
in the distant house, somewhere near but far. Packing,
perhaps. Folding neat underwear, sheathing cool silk
in a calm, green suitcase which travels well. He reaches
at last for the Welsh voices. Choral remedies –
can they suffice? He pauses, hands trembling, then bravely
inserts the CD. Perhaps he may yet be saved.

IV

Mr Philpott wakes in the blue bedroom. Beside him
Mrs Philpott dozes, her soft white shoulders curving
into dreams. Between the floral curtains, sun
spills from the conservatory, where saving
graces still are dancing. Sleepless, Philpott
counts his many losses. He has lost
his sons, his thin first wife, his confidence –
all of them gone. He turns to his cowrie shell
of safety, slipping one arm beneath her neck,
the other round her waist in the way she likes,
his skin breathing her in. Soon, he reflects,
there'll be toast and marmalade, the home-made, sweet-
bitter conserve of love. Ah George, she moans,
in her sleep. *George*. It is not his name.

V

George is not his name. But George isn't here – thus
Philpott consoles himself. Sadly he flies off
to sleep, airy and feathered. Mrs Philpott is dreaming
of pigs, a whole herd of them, and she's riding
the chief boar, clinging to yellow tusks. Spines cut
her inner thighs, searing the skin. Stop! she cries
but the ride goes harder, faster, until the brute
rears his huge head. It is George, her first husband:
he has got her now. Ah George, she pleads,
George – let me go. *No, no, by the hair on my
chinny chin chin*, he snaps, beard extended.
Almost too late, a white bird drops, enfolding her
in its wings. *You are voluptuous*, it sings. *Come.*
She embraces, weeping, the man who is holding her.

Julie O'Callaghan

HOGGING THE CHOW

I would love to know
who's hogging all the chow
down at that end.
It would interest me greatly.
Do I have to send a
SWAT team over there
to commandeer a few lumps of squash
and a handful of peas?
I seem to recall shelling out
for all this stuff.
Is that the smell of fried chicken in the air
or am I hallucinating
due to lack of nutrition?
My sainted wife
has been turned into stone
with her mouth hanging open
and a bowl of mashed potatoes
hovering three inches off the table.
Let's try banging our plates
with our cutlery.
It works in prison movies.

Dennis O'Driscoll

LIFE CYCLE
in memory of George Mackay Brown

January. Wind bellows. Stars hiss like smithy sparks.
The moon a snowball frozen in mid-flight.
George is rocking on his fireside chair.

February. The sea loud at the end of the street.
Ferries cancelled. Snowdrops seep through dampness.
George is sitting down to mutton broth.

March. Oystercatcher piping. Early tattie planting.
Gull-protected fishing boats wary of the equinoctial gales.
George is tired by now of his captivity.

April. Cloud boulders roll back from the Easter sun.
The tinker horse, a cuckoo, in the farmer's field.
George is taking the spring air on Brinkie's Brae.

May. Scissors-tailed swallows cut the tape, declare summer open.
A stray daddy-long-legs, unsteady on its feet as a new foal.
George is sampling home-brew from his vat.

June. Butterfly wings like ornamental shutters. Day scorches
down to diamonds, rubies before being lost at sea.
George is picnicking with friends on Rackwick beach.

July. Another wide-eyed sun. Its gold slick pours like oil
on the untroubled waves. Shoppers dab brows as they gossip.
George is drafting poems in a bottle-green shade.

August. Pudgy bees in romper suits suckled by flowers.
Well water rationed. Trout gills barely splashed.
George is hiding from the tourists' knock.

September. A brace of wrapped haddocks on the doorstep.
Mushrooms, snapped off under grass tufts, melt in the pan.
George is stocking up his shed with coal and peat.

October. Porridge and clapshot weather. Swan arrivals, divers.
Sun hangs, a smoking ham, suspended in the misty air.
George is ordering a hot dram at the pub.

November. Rain shaken out sideways like salt. Hail pebbles
flung against the window to announce winter's return.
George is adding a wool layer to his clothes.

December. Three strangers, bearing gifts, enquire the way
to byre and bairn. A brightness absent from the map of stars.
George's craft is grounded among kirkyard rocks.

Sharon Olds

The Talkers

All week, we talked. We talked
in the morning on the porch, when I combed my hair
and flung the comb-hair out into the air,
and it floated down the slope, toward the valley.
We talked while walking to the car, talked
over its mild, belled roof,
while opening the doors, then ducked down
and there we were, bent toward the interior, talking.
Meeting, in the middle of the day,
the first thing when we saw each other
we opened our mouths. All day,
we sang to each other the level music
of spoken language. Even while we ate
we did not pause, I'd speak to him through
the broken body of the butter cookie,
gently spraying him with crumbs. We talked
and walked, we leaned against the opposite sides of the
car and talked in the parking lot
until everyone else had driven off, we clung to its
dark cold raft and started a new subject.
We did not talk about his wife, much,
or my husband, but to everything else
we turned the workings of our lips and tongues
– up to our necks in the hot tub, or
walking up the steep road,
stepping into the hot dust as if
down into the ions of a wing, and on the
sand, next to each other, as we turned
the turns that upon each other would be the
turnings of joy – even under
water there trailed from our mouths the delicate
chains of our sentences. But mostly at night, and
far into the night, we talked until we

dropped, as if, stopping for an instant, we might
move right toward each other. Today,
he said he felt he could talk to me forever,
it must be the way angels live,
sitting across from each other, deep
in the bliss of their shared spirit. My God,
they are not going to touch each other.

Douglas Oliver

The Borrowed Bow

The moment stings, shorting like an old wireless
of bakelite body with a trellised raffia screen.
The shadowy corner's acrid with electricity,
blue air frazzed with black
in a cliffside house blank-windowed towards France.
But around the space of shock are other rooms
where old men, sitting by their wirelesses,
wear country check worsteds with a fleck of red
blodged with gravy. This moment
is a vanishing point on a post-war seacoast,
the pier blown up in case of German invasion.

The rooms still have that slow life
moving in them, a termite-gnawed Asante mask
on the walls of a retired colonial official,
an assegai from elsewhere in Africa,
a boot-polish shield, a bow, a poisoned arrow;
for there's an unexplored magic in all time,
a survival even now of a toothless mouth
sopping at a biscuit, a hand trembling
on a bony knee, about to reach
for porcelain on a frame of swivelling trays,
thin finger crooked as for a trigger.

I borrowed the bow of black hardwood,
took it and a bamboo stick into the garden.
Couldn't pull the leather string back;
the magic of the bow-spar wouldn't bend for me.
I knew I was just meddling. So I went indoors
to fiddle with the wireless innards:
electronic emotions and jerky excitements

in the village of valves, which cracked like gunfire,
a tracer arc streaked across dusty connections,
as if before the snap of it, the coil of smoke,
a tiny bow had shot a brilliant arrow.

Tom Paulin

DRUMCREE FOUR

The preacher
you know that costive overreacher
the mate of biblebashing lechers
says the Twelfth will be the settling
time then reaches
for his blackthorn
and marches to the barricade
– no more
flicks this time of the Orange Card
– they're in a tribal huff
it is a standoff

I listen to the radio
I read the papers
but how this caper
will end no one knows
only the word *settle*
its clanky its metallic
even archaic sound
hits the ear
like listening to a battered kettle
or a tin can
being kicked across a patch
of rocky ground
or concrete walkway
– should we cut an eyepatch
for the pirate preacher
then snap his stick?
he claims this patch of ground's
his tribe's alone
and through a megaphone
he gulders with a deep thick
ululating wheezing sound

that strains like Ulster
in a bulging holster
that bible uniform
pressed by what his father stuck
to – now watch the British state
as with fairness and no hate
it grasps the nettle
and says – walk? no way

Craig Raine

FROM A LA RECHERCHE DU TEMPS PERDU

So I turn to a dead language again:
ineo, I go into, enter, begin.

Doleo, I am in pain, I grieve.
And everyone thinks I am being brave.

Ignis, ignis, masculine, fire:
at St Pancras Crematorium, I stare,

light-headed with caffeine,
at the light-oak coffin,

wondering what I feel, where I stand.
Vulnus, vulneris, neuter, a wound.

I watch the coffin vanish
to Mozart on tape, its varnish

about to come up in blisters
and burst into a boa

of full-length, rustling fire,
just as we reach the Dies Irae.

Sinews shrink from the flames.
Sinews shrink in the flames.

I sentimentalise
and then revise.

Iter, itineris, neuter, a journey.
Without end. Where the road is empty.

Sine plus ablative, without.
The words are in my mouth

but I can't teach myself
the simple, difficult lesson of grief.

Too terrible to learn. Too hard
to have the words by heart.

I can't accept you're dead.
You're still here, in my head:

irritating, prickly, unsalved,
unsolved, unlovable, loved.

That bubble at the corner of your mouth.
Which seems somehow to mean so much.

Jeremy Reed

SITES

A warehouse burns in solid orange flame,
erupts at Bankside, a black cumulus
of tented smoke pyramiding the Thames.

He sits and contemplates biography,
a Persian carpet rages in the sky,
voluted purples peacocked into green,

a fuming skylight over Cannon Street.
A city's dawn is always visionary,
he strokes atomized stardust on his skin,

as though chasing gold embers from his pores.
His studio is torched. The years go by
memoried under bridges, blued with tears,

the same trains hustling into Charing Cross,
the changes registered inside his blood.
A day is like a pick-up which won't stay

faithful to anyone, despite the need
to have it open out into a friend.
Bugloss and borage present to his eyes . . .

He paces memory like it's a room
in which the furniture comes clear at dawn,
a blue vase loaded with redundant dreams,

a red one choked with flowers, he clears the lot
to know the moment, catch his breath again,
and feel the city fit him like a boot.

Adrian Rice

THE BIG PICTURE
for Raymond Armstrong

Outside the window,
B-movie rain falls in floods.
Someone must be on my roof,
Sending those buckets down.

Other hands have the house surrounded
With cranes and booms;
The gardens tracked,
The cameras dollying along.

While the key grip corners the gaffer,
The continuity girl works
With an awkward shoe,
And the best boy does what best boys do.

I suppose they are waiting on me.
Well, they can wait.
I'm not coming out.
What's happening is happening inside.

Maurice Riordan

Sky
the firmament sheweth His handiwork

Nothing much falls from the heavens, not in a day's walking
Or the night that follows, out here on the moors:
One shower of hail from the entirely blue, and now
The odd star burst that we think is comet dust
Igniting in the stratosphere – but nothing like
The skillet-size snowflakes that hit Matt Coleman's ranch
In '32; neither signs nor wonders,
Neither manna nor the Welshman's *pwdre ser*,
Never mind the parachute fifty years falling on Bodmin
Or the three suns – the Sun in Splendour! – that shone
On the eve of the Battle at Mortimer's Cross;
And nothing at all to compete with the asteroid-punch,
The lumpy planetestimal plucked from the Main Belt
Or the rugby ball booted mindlessly out of the Oort Cloud
That knocked the dinosaur off its ledge – not unless we
    start to think
Of the whole shebang taking a breather, a merciful lull,
In which the biochemical soup simmers
On the cosmic hob, while an inconspicuous quadruped,
With opposable thumbs and a nocturnal habit,
Goes on a blinder – leapfrogs from prey to hunter, from
    stalking
To husbandry, as brain and pelvic cavities egg each other on
Towards this tender equilibrium, this steady state
In which our soufflé spirits rise. Where nothing falls or spills,
Or not enough to sizzle the gently smouldering mass
Or collapse the mildly stinging air into a liquid bullet
And cancel one summer's night under the stars.

Carole Satyamurti

Gospel Oak to Barking, Barking to Gospel Oak:
the usual pleasures of the grubby train that shuffles
me to work and back include sinful snacks

novels in day-time. But not the raw
heaps of graveyard steel, urban farm
where everything moults in despair.

Nor terrace fronts whose every brick
is picked out in shaky black, or encrusted
from ground to eaves in multi-coloured mosaic.

My throat aches at the patience of it;
I think of my own, equally convinced, aesthetic.
Then, today, nature took sides and elected kitsch

throwing a vast canopy of flamy tatters
over the flatlands of east London. Brick,
glass, concrete reflected glory; altostratus

streaming in Strictly Ballroom rose,
Cartland mauve, Metro Goldwyn carmine
and russet – a brash brass band of a blaze.

At first, no one looked, but stared stiffly
at newspapers, slumped as if too full
of trouble to be touched; or as if

every day, Canary Wharf stood like a survivor
of *blitzkrieg*, and the sky spread out such gifts.
But then first one face then others came alive,

smiles passed between us as a flood
of copper, spilling across the reservoirs,
transformed greasy grey to dragon's blood.

Vernon Scannell

VIEWS AND DISTANCES

They sit together on their stolen towel
and count their few remaining francs and days
of dear vacation. Out in the bay the sea,
a crinkled spread of shimmering blue, sustains
an elegant white yacht at anchor there,
and, as they gaze, they see that, on the deck,
a man and woman have appeared who lean
languid at the vessel's rail and seem,
improbably, to offer stare for stare.

At night the sky's dark blue is deeper still,
is almost black. The rigging of the yacht
is hung with fairy-lights, and music drifts
and scents the air. The man in his white tux
and woman in her Dior gown still seem
to peer towards the shore as if they might
see once more the morning's teasing sight –
the enviable simplicities of youth
and deprivation, envy, appetite.

Pauline Stainer

CARAVAGGIO

Round the piazza
the boy apprentices
lie lip to lip.

Pigments pool in the hot shade,
cinnabar and narcotic green
numb to the touch.

Yesterday I stabbed a man.
Today I grind vermilion
for the Madonna of the Rosary

the light a cardsharp
always a trick ahead.

C K Stead

RAVIDUS THE BOOKMAN

Don't forget, Catullus
how that porker Ravidus
after his crisis
of lung and liver
(brought on he said
by the stress of a merger)
bounced right back,
left his job
as prince of publishers
to be literary editor
of a quality broadsheet
where he behaved
much as before
seldom reading books
(others did that) –
it was more a matter
of sniffing the wind
giving ear to gossip
having an eye for fashion
a feel for the market
and only now and then
hacking out a column
of consensus bookchat
in his execrable prose.

A hack is a hack is a
hack, says Cornelius
and I suppose he's right
but whenever did a Grub Street
penny-a-liner
sit above the clouds
in a comfortable chair
with a drink and headphones

doing the *Times* crossword
wondering where the hostess
with the lovely legs
spent her nights in New York –
and all on the profits
of other men's sweat?

Believe me, Cornelius
when lungs and liver
at last send Ravidus wailing
through streets of the city
down to where the dead men
write forever unpublished
those who bought him drinks
will piss on his name,
those who were indifferent
will forget it,
and another and another
and another Ravidus
will press and elbow forward
to fill his chair.

Anne Stevenson

MOONRISE

While my anxiety stood phoning you last evening,
My simpler self lay marvelling through glass
At the full moon marbling the clouds, climbing
In shafts, a headlamp through an underpass,
Until it swung free, cratered, deadly clear,
Earth's stillborn twin unsoiled by life or air.

And while our voices huddled mouth to ear,
I watched tenacity of long imagination
Cast her again in a film of the old goddess,
Chaste of the chase, more virgin than the Virgin,
Lifting herself from that rucked, unfeeling waste
As from the desert of her own ruined face.

Such an unhinging light. To see her. To see that.
As no one else had seen her. Or might see that.

David Sutton

Consider

Consider how they move, the galaxies,
Through the ocean of night like drift nets
Dragging deep space, though nothing we know is there
To be caught in that radiant star-knotted mesh.

Consider how they pass through one another
Like ghost armadas: let the stars be ships
A million miles apart: still that belittles
The loneliness of those bright galleons.

Consider light: by that same token see
A snail-track silverthreading black Saharas
Between the stars, yet nothing anywhere
Outpaces that immortal messenger.

And then consider: who shall know us, what
Companion us: in all the shadowed room
What hands might cup this candle, flickering
In time's wind, in the vast forever dark.

C K Williams

ICE

That astonishing thing that happens when you crack a needle-
    awl into a block of ice:
the way a perfect section through it crazes into gleaming fault-
    lines, fractures, facets;
dazzling silvery deltas that in one too-quick-to-capture instant
    madly complicate the cosmos of its innards.
Radiant now with spines and spikes, aggressive barbs of glittering
    light, a treasure hoard of light,
when you stab it again it comes apart in nearly equal segments,
    both faces grainy, gnawed at, dull.

An icehouse was a dark, low place of raw, unpainted wood,
always dank and black with melting ice.
There was sawdust and sawdust's tantalizing, half-sweet odor,
    which, so cold, seemed to pierce directly to the brain.
You'd step onto a low-roofed porch, someone would materialize,
take up great tongs and with precise, placating movements like a
    lion-tamer's slide an ice-block from its row.

Take the awl yourself now, thrust, and when the block splits do it
    again, yet again;
watch it disassemble into smaller fragments, crystal after fissured
    crystal.
Or if not the puncturing pick, try to make a metaphor, like Kafka's
    frozen sea within:
take into your arms the cake of actual ice, make a figure of its
    ponderous inertness,
of how its quickly wetting chill against your breast would frighten
    you and make you let it drop.

Imagine how even if it shattered and began to liquefy
the hope would still remain that if you quickly gathered up the
    slithery, perversely skittish chips,
they might be refrozen and the mass reconstituted, with precious
    little of its brilliance lost,
just this lucent shimmer on the rough, raised grain of water-
    rotten floor,
just this single drop, as sweet and warm as blood, evaporating on
    your tongue.

Frances Williams

OYSTER EATING

Luxury doesn't get more
Astringent. Plucked from
Cloudy depths, my plate
Of oysters wait for their
Moment, little glaciers
In silky cups. I suck

An avalanche of flesh.
Then clear my throat
Of their strange salt
Swallow, more touch
Than taste. Out of these
Rocky skulls, the brains

Come slippery as sex.
Each one tips over the
Rugged callused lips of
Its single shoe to speak
Only with the one tongue,
A probe both first and

Last. Such rash
Adventurers. Jonahs
In my whale. And also
Something sad in our
Hurried consummation.
A dozen down, I reach

A check-mate moment
In this game of numbers.
As Casanova, on a lucky
Night, might break a line
Of kisses, to pause for breath
On heaven's racing staircase.

Hugo Williams

Bar Italia

How beautiful it would be to wait for you again
in the usual place,
not looking at the door,
keeping a lookout in the long mirror,
knowing that if you are late
it will not be too late,
knowing that all I have to do
is wait a little longer
and you will be pushing through the other customers,
out of breath, apologetic.
Where have you been, for God's sake?
I was starting to worry.

How long did we say we would wait
if one of us was held up?
It's been so long and still no sign of you.
As time goes by, I search other faces in the bar,
rearranging their features
until they are monstrous versions of you,
their heads wobbling from side to side
like heads on sticks.
Your absence inches forward
until it is standing next to me.
Now it has taken the seat I was saving.
Now we are face to face in the long mirror.

Cliff Yates

CLARA

'Sweet, Sir?' 'No thank you. I've just eaten
a little boy.' He stands at the classroom door,

rubbing together big hands. 'Poetry
tomorrow Clara. Poetry!' Clara

has other plans. She's seeing Andy who's
doing Sociology and English at the Tech. Saturday

he took her on the terraces, Villa Park.
She stood behind him, warming her hands

in the back pockets of his Wranglers.
Later they shared a hot dog at the fair,

started at either end, met in the middle.
On the bus home they sat upstairs at the back,

smoking French cigarettes. He cupped both hands
around her goldfish in its plastic bag.

She peeped through the cracks, wanting it to sleep
in the pink dark. Tomorrow it's his place;

his mum's out for the day. He'll read her
his essay on *The Crisis of Identity of the Post*

Industrial British Working Class. They'll lie
together in front of the electric fire,

listening to Van Morrison. Later, upstairs,
they'll run a warm bath, set the goldfish free.